100
Jane Austen
Cryptograms

By Bookprism Puzzles

© 2019

Table of Contents

Cryptograms · 3

Cryptogram Solutions · 32

Cryptograms

We've taken 100 classic lines from the novels of Jane Austen and scrambled them by replacing each letter with another. It's up to you to decrypt the lines by figuring out which letters replace which.

Don't worry: You've got hints on the next few pages to get you started, and we've identified the novel each line comes from.

Good luck!

1: U=A
2: I=O
3: K=T
4: D=E
5: O=E
6: U=T
7: L=O
8: H=I
9: I=T
10: A=H
11: M=O
12: L=A
13: O=A
14: N=I
15: K=E
16: N=I
17: A=N
18: C=E
19: Y=N
20: F=A
21: B=I
22: K=O
23: M=S
24: M=T
25: M=T
26: C=T
27: K=T
28: V=I
29: G=O
30: Y=N
31: J=H
32: K=I
33: X=O
34: S=T
35: Q=A
36: C=E
37: I=N
38: B=S
39: G=I
40: Q=O
41: K=S
42: S=E
43: Q=O
44: T=E
45: I=O
46: J=N
47: Y=O
48: P=O

49: A=T	73: W=T
50: O=I	74: H=I
51: Z=A	75: E=N
52: J=O	76: C=A
53: Q=A	77: B=A
54: P=H	78: I=A
55: B=E	79: S=H
56: F=E	80: B=R
57: B=N	81: Z=T
58: D=A	82: O=T
59: N=O	83: M=E
60: F=A	84: N=O
61: F=O	85: R=E
62: N=E	86: A=O
63: T=I	87: O=T
64: S=T	88: D=A
65: M=E	89: O=E
66: F=S	90: S=E
67: F=I	91: G=I
68: D=O	92: B=O
69: V=A	93: D=I
70: S=E	94: V=T
71: T=E	95: R=N
72: C=N	96: Q=E

97: U=E
98: H=E
99: W=T
100: Q=O

1. Sense and Sensibility

OG OVQ'G BNUG BC VUT WM GNOQI GNUG ZCSOQCV XV,
It isn't what we say or think that defines us,

RXG BNUG BC ZW.
but what we do.

. . . .

2. Emma

TIG AGVD CX DLX CXVD OGNKX IS TIGY IZR
You must be the best judge of your own

LUJJFRXVV.
happiness.

. . . .

3. Pride and Prejudice

PLK FUDFNU KEUWBUNMUB JNKUZ BD WLTE, KEJK
But people themselves alter so much, that

KEUZU RB BDWUKERXS XUQ KD PU DPBUZMUG RX KEUW
there is something new to be observed in them

HDZ UMUZ.
for ever.

. . . .

4. Pride and Prejudice

KD RJ G VDOLBDWGO, GOC R GW G VDOLBDWGO'J
He is a gentleman, and I am a gentleman's

CGHVKLDM. JS QGM ED GMD DYHGB.
daughter. So far we are equal.

. . . .

5. Sense and Sensibility

It is not what we think or feel that makes us

DW DU QVW PRFW PO WRDQX VZ HOOG WRFW SFXOU CU

who we are; it is what we do or fail to do.

PRV PO FZO. DW DU PRFW PO BV: VZ HFDG WV BV...

. . . .

6. Persuasion

Dare not say that man forgets sooner than

GLBC MQU ZLT UOLU HLM KQBNCUZ ZQQMCB UOLM

woman, that his love has an earlier death.

EQHLM, UOLU OPZ XQAC OLZ LM CLBXPCB GCLUO.

. . . .

7. Northanger Abbey

The person, be it gentleman or lady, who

DFZ YZGQLB, CZ AD WZBDOZSKB LG OKJM, RFL

has not pleasure in a good novel, must be

FKQ BLD YOZKQHGZ AB K WLLJ BLNZO, SHQD CZ

intolerably stupid.

ABDLOZGKCOM QDHYAJ.

. . . .

8. Lady Susan

There is exquisite pleasure in subduing

WBZKZ HC ZSLNHCHWZ GYZFCNKZ HD CNAVNHDJ

an insolent spirit, in making a person

FD HDCXYZDW CGHKHW, HD TFQHDJ F GZKCXD

pre-determined to dislike acknowledge

GKZ-VZWZKTHDZV WX VHCYHQZ, FUQDXMYZVJZ

one's superiority.

XDZ'C CNGZKHXKHWE.

. . . .

9. Northanger Abbey

If I could not be persuaded into doing
UA U PDKNT GDI WR CRSXKHTRT UGID TDUGQ
what I thought wrong, I will never be tricked
YMHI U IMDKQMI YSDGQ, U YUNN GRERS WR ISUPFRT
into it.
UGID UI.

. . . .

10. Mansfield Park

Those who have not love must be satisfied with
RAFHS VAF AZNS GFR OFJS OMHR WS HZREHXESI VERA
what they have.
VAZR RASK AZNS.

. . . .

11. Emma

There are people, who the more you do for
UOPNP CNP TPMTJP, ROM UOP BMNP EMD VM WMN
them, the less they will do for themselves.
UOPB, UOP JPKK UOPE RLJJ VM WMN UOPBKPJYPK.

. . . .

12. Sense and Sensibility

I have not wanted syllables where
P TLWC OBG XLOGCV QSJJLUJCQ XTCMC
actions have spoken so plainly.
LIGPBOQ TLWC QABYCO QB AJLPOJS.

. . . .

13. Mansfield Park

IF THIS MAN HAD NOT TWELVE THOUSAND A
VW SNVA HOZ NOX ZMS SJRDQR SNMTAOZX O

YEAR, HE WOULD BE A VERY STUPID FELLOW.
CROB, NR JMTDX UR O QRBC ASTEVX WRDDMJ.

. . . .

14. Northanger Abbey

FRIENDSHIP IS REALLY THE FINEST BALM FOR THE
KYNSCRMWNQ NM YSTVVP DWS KNCSMD OTVF KIY DWS

PANGS OF DISAPPOINTED LOVE.
QTCZM IK RNMTQQINCDSR VIUS.

. . . .

15. Mansfield Park

LIFE SEEMS BUT A QUICK SUCCESSION OF BUSY
ZLBK UKKJU GDW T NDLOP UDOOKUULAS AB GDUE

NOTHINGS.
SAWRLSMU.

. . . .

16. Mansfield Park

A LARGE INCOME IS THE BEST RECIPE FOR
E CEBKO NSXQGO NF WZO IOFW BOXNYO UQB

HAPPINESS I EVER HEARD OF.
ZEYYNSOFF N ODOB ZOEBL QU.

. . . .

17. Pride and Prejudice

IT IS A TRUTH UNIVERSALLY
SJ SV H JBPJO PASUCBVHMMK

ACKNOWLEDGED, THAT A SINGLE MAN IN
HDLATFMCNZCN, JOHJ H VSAZMC XHA SA

POSSESSION OF A GOOD FORTUNE, MUST BE IN
QTVVCVVSTA TI H ZTTN ITBJPAC, XPVJ EC SA

WANT OF A WIFE.
FHAJ TI H FSIC.

. . . .

18. Emma

SHE WAS HAPPY, SHE KNEW SHE WAS HAPPY, AND
NSC ION SOXXT, NSC BYCI NSC ION SOXXT, OYL

KNEW SHE OUGHT TO BE HAPPY.
BYCI NSC QHRSV VQ PC SOXXT.

. . . .

19. Pride and Prejudice

THE DISTANCE IS NOTHING WHEN ONE HAS A MOTIVE.
GAU RWCGFYXU WC YKGAWYH MAUY KYU AFC F SKGWZU.

. . . .

20. Emma

I CANNOT MAKE SPEECHES, EMMA IF I LOVED YOU
B MFQQHI CFNA PSAAMYAP, ACCF...BV B UHZAR OHX

LESS, I MIGHT BE ABLE TO TALK ABOUT IT MORE.
UAPP, B CBKYI LA FLUA IH IFUN FLHXI BI CHDA.

. . . .

21. Emma

Without music, life would be a blank to me.

SBFOYDF ZDEBG, JBTA SYDJQ KA I KJIPR FY ZA.

....

22. Sense and Sensibility

Life could do nothing for her, beyond giving time for a better preparation for death.

WCYS XKDWV VK AKOTCAJ YKP TSP, MSZKAV JCBCAJ OCUS YKP G MSOOSP LPSLGPGOCKA YKP VSGOT.

....

23. Sense and Sensibility

I wish, as well as everybody else, to be perfectly happy; but, like everybody else, it must be in my own way.

V KVMN, ZM KYPP ZM YCYTQHILQ YPMY, EI HY XYTSYBEPQ NZXXQ; HAE, PVWY YCYTQHILQ YPMY, VE JAME HY VD JQ IKD KZQ.

....

24. Mansfield Park

I was quiet, but I was not blind.

C RBK DTCHM, ITM C RBK VJM ISCVX.

....

25. Sense and Sensibility

To wish was to hope, and to hope was to expect.

MH QKOC QNO MH CHAS, NUV MH CHAS QNO MH SGASZM.

26. Persuasion

Let us never underestimate the
BIC LA XIKIM LXEIMIACZQPCI CWI
power of a well-written letter.
NJTIM JH P TIBB-TMZCCIX BICCIM.

27. Mansfield Park

But there certainly are not so many men of
HMK KFDLD ODLKZNGUX ZLD GAK JA YZGX YDG AW
large fortune in the world as there are
UZLED WALKMGD NG KFD TALUC ZJ KFDLD ZLD
pretty women to deserve them.
BLDKKX TAYDG KA CDJDLQD KFDY.

28. Emma

Nobody who has not been in the interior of a
AHWHLB, SYH YCF AHD WMMA VA DYM VADMKVHK HR C
family, can say what the difficulties of any
RCTVIB, GCA FCB SYCD DYM LVRRVGJIDVMF HR CAB
individual of that family may be.
VALVNVLJCI HR DYCD RCTVIB TCB WM.

29. Pride and Prejudice

RGN ENPQ HAVTM PGEA GK ER IDCHGPGIDR. QDCMY
You must learn some of my philosophy. Think

GMHR GK QDA IVPQ VP CQP TAEAEUTVMFA OCBAP RGN
only of the past as its remembrance gives you

IHAVPNTA.
pleasure.

. . . .

30. Sense and Sensibility

V YXHXW GVKO JP PEEXYM, FZJ V NC KP EPPAVKOAS
I never wish to offend, but I am so foolishly

KOS, JONJ V PEJXY KXXC YXTAVTXYJ, GOXY V NC
shy, that I often seem negligent, when I am

PYAS RXDJ FNIR FS CS YNJZWNA NGRGNWMYXKK.
only kept back by my natural awkwardness.

. . . .

31. Mansfield Park

JWP RXH EJRVNJEU QHC PWAKWTEDRHU XWPW
Her own thoughts and reflections were

JQLDEVQKKM JWP LWUE TRFGQHDRHU.
habitually her best companions.

. . . .

32. Sense and Sensibility

ZCPGO UTP CPYO NKWG DTVVKPGII XDGBG HDGBG
Money can only give happiness where there

KI PCHDKPN GYIG HC NKWG KH.
is nothing else to give it.

. . . .

33. Persuasion

How quick come the reasons for approving
KXR NWFUV UXET GKT PTSMXCM ZXP SYYPXDFCO
what we like.
RKSG RT BFVT.

. . . .

34. Pride and Prejudice

There is a stubbornness about me that never
SCLHL YO X OSZGGUHEELOO XGUZS PL SCXS ELRLH
can bear to be frightened at the will
QXE GLXH SU GL WHYICSLELJ XS SCL DYFF
of others. My courage always rises at every
UW USCLHO. PA QUZHXIL XFDXAO HYOLO XS LRLHA
attempt to intimidate me.
XSSLPMS SU YESYPYJXSL PL.

. . . .

35. Pride and Prejudice

Oh, Lizzy! Do anything rather than marry
IM, SYBBE! JI QFEGMYFU TQGMZT GMQF HQTTE
without affection.
OYGMIWG QPPZVGYIF.

. . . .

36. Mansfield Park

I think it ought not to be set down as
V HLVOS VH BINLH OBH HB ZC UCH QBRO MU
certain, that a man must be acceptable to
XCDHMVO, HLMH M AMO AIUH ZC MXXCTHMZYC HB
every woman he may happen to know himself.
CWCDG RBAMO LC AMG LMTTCO HB YVSC LVAUCYK.

. . . .

37. Emma

I don't approve of surprises. The

B JDI'Y RMMSDGZ DQ TFSMSBTZT. YCZ

pleasure is never enhanced and the

MPZRTFSZ BT IZGZS ZICRIOZJ RIJ YCZ

inconvenience is considerable.

BIODIGZIBZIOZ BT ODITBJSRNPZ.

. . . .

38. Mansfield Park

Every moment has its pleasures and its

SESYL CFCSVW QDB AWB HGSDBRYSB DVZ AWB

hope.

QFHS.

. . . .

39. Lady Susan

Where there is a disposition to

...KZFQF BZFQF GX P MGXOJXGBGJE BJ

dislike, a motive will never be wanting.

MGXHGUF, P TJBGAF KGHH EFAFQ LF KPEBGED.

. . . .

40. Sense and Sensibility

A man who has nothing to do with his own time

B ZBP MSQ SBY PQWSUPI WQ RQ MUWS SUY QMP WUZH

has no conscience in his intrusion on that

SBY PQ JQPYJUHPJH UP SUY UPWOVYUQP QP WSBW

of others.

QE QWSHOY.

. . . .

41. Emma

Evil to some is always good to others.

NOEG PL KLFN EK MGHMBK XLLW PL LPYNQK.

....

42. Sense and Sensibility

I will be calm. I will be mistress of myself.

U RUEE IS ODEW. U RUEE IS WUHGXSHH FA WPHSEA.

....

43. Emma

Vanity working on a weak head produces every sort of mischief.

HNCSFI TQBYSCR QC N TMNY AMNU GBQUPOMX MHMBI XQBF QV ESXOASMV.

....

44. Pride and Prejudice

Angry people are not always wise.

ISUJO GTHGKT IJT SHX IKLIOZ LEZT.

....

45. Northanger Abbey

Beware how you give your heart.

DQKCTQ FIK EIM PSBQ EIMT FQCTH.

. . . .

46. Pride and Prejudice

To be fond of dancing was a certain step

MA GW CAJX AC XDJHSJT YDV D HWZMDSJ VMWI

towards falling in love.

MAYDZXV CDEESJT SJ EAFW.

. . . .

47. Sense and Sensibility

The more I know of the world, the more I am

RXV AYOV Q NMYJ YU RXV JYOFC, RXV AYOV Q TA

convinced that I shall never see a man whom I

IYMBQMIVC RXTR Q PXTFF MVBVO PVV T ATM JXYA Q

can really love. I require so much.

ITM OVTFFZ FYBV. Q OVWDQOV PY ADIX!

. . . .

48. Pride and Prejudice

A lady's imagination is very rapid; it jumps

O TOCK'G DFOWDROMDPR DG QSHK HOLDC; DM XYFLG

from admiration to love, from love to

EHPF OCFDHOMDPR MP TPQS, EHPF TPQS MP

matrimony in a moment.

FOMHDFPRK DR O FPFSRM.

. . . .

49. Sense and Sensibility

WC AWCJ PCRTGACP, AI HTLC WXHNCQK NAXQQ
HE THEN DEPARTED, TO MAKE HIMSELF STILL

HIGC XJACGCNAXJO, XJ AWC HXPNA IK T WCTMD
MORE INTERESTING, IN THE MIDST OF A HEAVY

GTXJ.
RAIN.

. . . .

50. Sense and Sensibility

OI O QUJXB SJE PVUK FOY FMDTE, MAMTREFOVN
IF I COULD BUT KNOW HIS HEART, EVERYTHING

KUJXB SMQUGM MDYR.
WOULD BECOME EASY.

. . . .

51. Pride and Prejudice

KI ZGG RXUK WAB LU JI Z NHUTC, TXNGIZVZXL VUHL
WE ALL KNOW HIM TO BE A PROUD, UNPLEASANT SORT

UY BZX; JTL LWAV KUTGC JI XULWAXE AY DUT
OF MAN; BUT IT IS WOULD BE NOTHING OF YOU

HIZGGD GARIC WAB.
REALLY LOVED HIM.

. . . .

52. Lady Susan

E IG VENZB JC WLUGEVVEXM GO DESS VJ VTZ

YIRNEYZW JC JVTZNWJC NZWEMXEXM GO JDX

ALBMZGZXV EX BZCZNZXYZ VJ VTJWZ VJ DTJG E JDZ

XJ BLVO, IXB CJN DTJG E CZZS XJ NZWRZYV.

. . . .

53. Emma

METSNPZNXX EX QCMQLX METSNPZNXX, HDU WRCCL EX ZRU QCMQLX WRCCL.

....

54. Persuasion

NHHX PWVXB LPX PNB WCZTRFXB ZPX NJX WY ITCLPRHJ; ICZ ZPX NJX WY XUWZRWH LPX DXEZNRHTM PNB HWZ.

....

55. Emma

D LUMTAB EQYDM, QK TQQN KQPGFMB, UL DAEDOL *A SINGLE WOMAN OF GOOD FORTUNE, IS ALWAYS*
PBLWBXGDCAB, DMN YDO CB DL LBMLUCAB DMN *RESPECTABLE, AND MAY BE AS SENSIBLE AND*
WABDLDMG DL DMO CQNO BALB. *PLEASANT AS ANY BODY ELSE.*

....

56. Lady Susan

XSN NWHN PVRHC GY H OVVI GCZFFZ PWV, PWGIF GCYSINFZ XQ HTTSYHNGVC, THC XF PVJLFZ VC XQ TVRMIGRFCNY.

....

57. Pride and Prejudice

I HAVE NOT THE PLEASURE OF UNDERSTANDING YOU.

L VRAQ BWJ JVQ OZQRGDHQ WC DBXQHGJRBXLBE UWD.

....

58. Pride and Prejudice

I AM HAPPIER EVEN THAN JANE; SHE ONLY SMILES,

S DJ EDTTSGB GLGU NEDU IDUG; AEG HUOP AJSOGA,

I LAUGH.

S ODMYE.

....

59. Pride and Prejudice

I WRITE ONLY TO BID YOU FAREWELL. THE SPELL IS

X MSXCW NZJP CN HXV PNA DBSWMWJJ. CGW TQWJJ XT

REMOVED; I SEE YOU AS YOU ARE.

SWLNUWV; X TWW PNA BT PNA BSW.

....

60. Persuasion

IF THERE IS ANY THING DISAGREEABLE GOING ON,

YT QRJKJ YL FPH QRYPN XYLFNKJJFVBJ NWYPN WP,

MEN ARE ALWAYS SURE TO GET OUT OF IT

ZJP FKJ FBSFHL LGKJ QW NJQ WGQ WT YQ.

....

61. Emma

FKZ JOYQ FQ MJZ DFUYI XOKKFM BKIZURMOKI MJZ LYZORBUZR FQ MJZ FMJZU.

. . . .

62. Pride and Prejudice

A JTXN INNV T ZNYPAZJ INAVH TYY QD YAPN, AV FMTKUAKN, UJSRHJ VSU AV FMAVKAFYN.

. . . .

63. Emma

TQZDDZ, T FA JDYM CHYYM IH VD YTWEI TQ IETC TQCIFQPD. T SHKBZ AKPE YFIEDY EFJD VDDQ ADYYM IEFQ STCD.

. . . .

64. Northanger Abbey

KS EUNDKEUA DVIMJJMV ASUXWKVUAA MQ EUXAMV SM EUAKAS SCU XSSEXISKMV MQ ZUKVY IXBBUW SCU JMAS ICXEJKVY YKEB KV SCU PMEBW.

. . . .

65. Persuasion

S JROM OL JMRN KLW ORZG RALWO RZZ HLYMU RI SB OJMK HMNM BSUM ZRVSMI SUIOMRV LB NROSLURZ XNMROWNMI. ULUM LB WI HRUO OL AM SU XRZY HROMNI RZZ LWN ZSQMI.

. . . .

66. Mansfield Park

FAXQZFBIAFF DCFJ KXUKTF MA QPHSZWAI TPC VIPU, MANKCFA JBAHA ZF IP BPLA PQ K NCHA.

. . . .

67. Lady Susan

F BSKJ RWZ EJZ ZASRHDFYYFPJL CEPJYO JRWDVB ZW PJJ OAJLJAFIS.

. . . .

68. Persuasion

PTXKX ADOBW TJYX CXXV VD PMD TXJKPQ QD DEXV, VD PJQPXQ QD QGIGBJK, VD ZXXBGVSQ QD GV OVGQDV.

. . . .

69. **Pride and Prejudice**

S NFXOVYF VLGFY VOO GZFYF SU PQ FPRQATFPG OSMF YFVNSPJ!

....

70. **Persuasion**

VYS LKY'O ZKAO LKA WS KO QVVI KO KYVCGSJ'O, WRC ZS KFF FMUS VRJ VZY WSOC.

....

71. **Northanger Abbey**

YC! M VK WTSMBCRTW IMRC RCT PYYG! M UCYHSW SMGT RY UZTEW KX ICYST SMAT ME QTVWMEB MR.

....

72. **Northanger Abbey**

W IZCCGA DJBZN KBRR BCGMSV AG PB MCWCABRRWSWPRB.

....

73. Persuasion

A QIYXSYZWDC MUGYIJY WTPW MZY BIYWWC QPEY HMSDR UY QMDDMHYR UC QAJY PZR WTAIWC QIAKTWG.

....

74. Mansfield Park

ZJC IUZ KCCYHFP, RJHFBHFP, RQCGOYHFP UOTXR CLCQARJHFP; UPHRURCE, JUSSA, GHZCQUOYC, HFKHFHRCYA TOYHPCE, UOZTYXRCYA UFPQA.

....

75. Mansfield Park

M VYESEWCC VYH HWMSDEF, QHYQWHIR SDHWZAWS, ULCA GW ME WSLZMADYE DE DACWIV.

....

76. Sense and Sensibility

ERHX GHVP HXR ICKKBRYMM. GHV XCRL RHLIBRD UVL KCLBYRJY- HP DBOY BL C FHPY NCMJBRCLBRD RCFY, JCWW BL IHKY.

....

77. Pride and Prejudice

UR'W NFFV SBVD DFBOW WUVIF U JBT WQIJ BV FYFSKZBOD XFHFRBNZF.

....

78. Northanger Abbey

SZJTJ XJQXRJ ITJ TJIRRU IWWIBZJN, XQKJTWU OWGJRD OG SJIRWZ.

....

79. Northanger Abbey

USA SXT JYKSGJR KY TY LHK KY CYERGOA SAEUAVC XJT LA SXWWGAE KSXJ AOAE

....

80. Pride and Prejudice

TDB EWXO CD EL HPNL, SGO OD FXRL KADBO TDB DGB QLPIWSDBK, XQC HXGIW XO OWLF PQ DGB OGBQ?

....

81. Mansfield Park

HN RWMN WCC W KNZZNF EYDXN DU PYFJNCMNJ, DT HN HPYCX WZZNUX ZP DZ, ZRWU WUS PZRNF GNFJPU LWU KN.

....

82. Mansfield Park

J NJOAD KE JINJBE OVV RJEO VZ OVV EIVN. K AJWWVO UT HKAOJOTH OV UB J NJOAD.

....

83. Mansfield Park

MKMAOZEUO VNFMX DE JE DPMNA ERT RWODE HPEEXM DPMNA ERT DNBM WTU BWTTMA EL UMKEDNET.

....

84. Emma

QJS ZNLQ YFINZKASJSFLYDPS QJYFO YF QJS RNAPT QN G ZGF, YL G RNZGF RJN ASXSIQL JYL NWWSA NW ZGAAYGOS!

....

85. Northanger Abbey

ANRQR WG JSANWJK W HSZEI JSA IS VSQ ANSGR HNS PQR QRPEEO CO VQWRJIG. W NPUR JS JSAWSJ SV ESUWJK MRSMER TO NPEURG, WA WG JSA CO JPAZQR.

....

86. Mansfield Park

AU RAEVWN K JAMN FNV, CEQ QFNVN GVN GW DGZX UAVDW AU JAMN GW QFNVN GVN DADNZQW KZ QKDN.

....

87. Emma

L IXRIWD CFDFSZF OKF GFDO OSFIOVFUO GFQIBDF L UFZFS MBO BM RLOK IUW AOKFS.

....

88. Sense and Sensibility

JTCJKT DKLDSR KUET BCI TETI LXTM ZXTIT UR DM DMMWUZS ZC QT JDUO ZXTH.

....

89. Persuasion

F IFM UGOL MGB AOYGXOA SAGI LRYK UOXGBJGM GS BKO KOFAB BG LRYK F DGIFM! KO GREKB MGB; KO UGOL MGB.

....

90. Pride and Prejudice

OFH YHBV NTTFD YS VF VSTT OFH XFD NUZSQVTO K NZYKUS NQZ TFWS OFH.

....

91. Lady Susan

G IWXDD PQPE BPIFGIP SWP NXL JWM YXL VP HEXSGAGPB VR SWP FXIIGML JWGYW WP LPQPE JGIWPB SM GLIFGEP, LME IMDGYGSPB SWP XQMJXD MA.

....

92. Sense and Sensibility

RQ D VBBI RE LCTT LZRUUCS, R DTLDAE QRSO RU UBB EKBZU.

....

93. **Emma**

MDKKT HJDFNM BR SWQMW HR UW MDKKT DL HJWT QAW BRFW UT MWFMDUKW VWRVKW DF QF DPVZBWFH EQT.

. . . .

94. **Pride and Prejudice**

P NSAV HXWIG VB JX KBGVXGV RPVD JXPGM DWFFPXI VDWG P ZXAXIQX.

. . . .

95. **Emma**

ZL GJZRDB OHY DIZRD SRGIFOHVPQ IRY EIRGJ, GJYQ OHY BSHY GI EYRV GJY RYKG.

. . . .

96. **Emma**

NQUUQX NQ EGUJKOU RQHRQ UJZH VGRZYYDP GU ZR PKO WK.

. . . .

97. Pride and Prejudice

FDPDGM HRF QUWW ONRQ Z VYEEUB! PYQ ZQ ZV RWORMV VD. QNDVU OND GD FDQ HDKXWRZF RBU FUCUB XZQZUG.

. . . .

98. Sense and Sensibility

XAS SY EOOHED FEOOG LFHM W EI QY IWQHDEXCH YF! LFY NEM DHBAWDH WS?

. . . .

99. Emma

WBVF CBEE MFSFJKEEG EFHHFS WUF BSWFJFHW NT FLFJG KWWKRUVFSW SNW CBWUBS WUF ZKBEG RBJREF.

. . . .

100. Mansfield Park

HQA WMCN ZAMYKIKNR EWKJW K WMG SQI UNOQVN RAXXQRNG IQ NLKRI KS RAJW M GNTVNN KS MSH WADMS JVNMIAVN. HQA WMCN RQDN IQAJWNR QO IWN MSTNY KS HQA.

. . . .

Cryptogram Solutions

1.

It isn't what we say or think that defines us, but what we do.

2.

You must be the best judge of your own happiness.

3.

But people themselves alter so much, that there is something new to be observed in them for ever.

4.

He is a gentleman, and I am a gentleman's daughter. So far we are equal.

5.

It is not what we think or feel that makes us who we are. It is what we do. Or fail to do...

6.

Dare not say that man forgets sooner than woman, that his love has an earlier death.

7.

The person, be it gentleman or lady, who has not pleasure in a good novel, must be intolerably stupid.

8.

There is exquisite pleasure in subduing an insolent spirit, in making a person pre-determined to dislike, acknowledge one's superiority.

9.

If I could not be persuaded into doing

what I thought wrong, I will never be tricked

into it.

10.

Those who have not more must be satisfied with

what they have.

11.

There are people, who the more you do for

them, the less they will do for themselves.

12.

I have not wanted syllables where

actions have spoken so plainly.

13.

If this man had not twelve thousand a year, he would be a very stupid fellow.

14.

Friendship is really the finest balm for the pangs of disappointed love.

15.

Life seems but a quick succession of busy nothings.

16.

A large income is the best recipe for happiness I ever heard of.

17.

It is a truth universally acknowledged, that a single man in possession of a good fortune, must be in want of a wife.

18.

She was happy, she knew she was happy, and knew she ought to be happy.

19.

The distance is nothing when one has a motive.

20.

I cannot make speeches, Emma...If I loved you less, I might be able to talk about it more.

21.

Without music, life would be a blank to me.

22.

Life could do nothing for her, beyond giving time for a better preparation for death.

23.

I wish, as well as everybody else, to be perfectly happy; but, like everybody else, it must be in my own way.

24.

I was quiet, but I was not blind.

25.

To wish was to hope, and to hope was to expect.

26.

Let us never underestimate the power of a well-written letter.

27.

But there certainly are not so many men of large fortune in the world as there are pretty women to deserve them.

28.

Nobody, who has not been in the interior of a family, can say what the difficulties of any individual of that family may be.

29.

You must learn some of my philosophy. Think only of the past as its remembrance gives you pleasure.

30.

I never wish to offend, but I am so foolishly shy, that I often seem negligent, when I am only kept back by my natural awkwardness.

31.

Her own thoughts and reflections were habitually her best companions.

32.

Money can only give happiness where there is nothing else to give it.

33.

How quick come the reasons for approving what we like.

34.

There is a stubbornness about me that never can bear to be frightened at the will of others. My courage always rises at every attempt to intimidate me.

35.

Oh, Lizzy! do anything rather than marry without affection.

36.

I think it ought not to be set down as certain, that a man must be acceptable to every woman he may happen to like himself.

37.

I don't approve of surprises. The pleasure is never enhanced and the inconvenience is considerable.

38.

Every moment has its pleasures and its hope.

39.

...where there is a disposition to dislike, a motive will never be wanting.

40.

A man who has nothing to do with his own time has no conscience in his intrusion on that of others.

41.

Evil to some is always good to others.

42.

I will be calm. I will be mistress of myself.

43.

Vanity working on a weak head produces every sort of mischief.

44.

Angry people are not always wise.

45.

Beware how you give your heart.

46.

To be fond of dancing was a certain step towards falling in love.

47.

The more I know of the world, the more I am convinced that I shall never see a man whom I can really love. I require so much!

48.

A lady's imagination is very rapid; it jumps from admiration to love, from love to matrimony in a moment.

49.

He then departed, to make himself still more interesting, in the midst of a heavy rain.

50.

If I could but know his heart, everything would become easy.

51.

We all know him to be a proud, unpleasant sort of man; but this would be nothing if you really liked him.

52.

I am tired of submitting my will to the caprices of othersof resigning my own judgement in deference to those to whom I owe no duty, and for whom I feel no respect.

53.

Wickedness is always wickedness, but folly is not always folly.

54.

Anne hoped she had outlived the age of blushing; but the age of emotion she certainly had not.

55.

A single woman, of good fortune, is always respectable, and may be as sensible and pleasant as any body else.

56.

But that woman is a fool indeed who, while insulted by accusation, can be worked on by compliments.

57.

I have not the pleasure of understanding you.

58.

I am happier even than Jane; she only smiles, I laugh.

59.

I write only to bid you Farewell. The spell is removed; I see you as you are.

60.

If there is any thing disagreeable going on, men are always sure to get out of it.

61.

One half of the world cannot understand the pleasures of the other.

62.

I have been a selfish being all my life, in practice, though not in principle.

63.

Indeed, I am very sorry to be right in this instance. I would much rather have been merry than wise.

64.

It requires uncommon steadiness of reason to resist the attraction of being called the most charming girl in the world.

65.

I hate to hear you talk about all women as if they were fine ladies instead of rational creatures. None of us want to be in calm waters all our lives.

66.

Selfishness must always be forgiven you know, because there is no hope of a cure.

67.

I have not yet tranquillised myself enough to see Frederica.

68.

There could have been no two hearts so open, no tastes so similar, no feelings so in unison.

69.

I declare after all there is no enjoyment like reading!

70.

One man's ways may be as good as another's, but we all like our own best.

71.

Oh! I am delighted with the book! I should like to spend my whole life in reading it.

72.

I cannot speak well enough to be unintelligible.

73.

I frequently observe that one pretty face would be followed by five and thirty frights.

74.

She was feeling, thinking, trembling about everything; agitated, happy, miserable, infinitely obliged, absolutely angry.

75.

A fondness for reading, properly directed, must be an education in itself.

76.

Know your own happiness. You want nothing but patience- or give it a more fascinating name, call it hope.

77.

It's been many years since I had such an exemplary vegetable.

78.

Where people are really attached, poverty itself is wealth.

79.

she had nothing to do but to forgive herself and be happier than ever

80.

For what do we live, but to make sport for our neighbors, and laugh at them in our turn?

81.

We have all a better guide in ourselves, if we would attend to it, than any other person can be.

82.

A watch is always too fast or too slow. I cannot be dictated to by a watch.

83.

Everybody likes to go their own way to choose their own time and manner of devotion.

84.

The most incomprehensible thing in the world to a man, is a woman who rejects his offer of marriage!

85.

There is nothing I would not do for those who are really my friends. I have no notion of loving people by halves, it is not my nature.

86.

Of course I love her, but there are as many forms of love as there are moments in time.

87.

I always deserve the best treatment because I never put up with any other.

88.

People always live for ever when there is an annuity to be paid them.

89.

A man does not recover from such devotion of the heart to such a woman! He ought not; he does not.

90.

You must allow me to tell you how ardently I admire and love you.

91.

I shall ever despise the man who can be gratified by the passion which he never wished to inspire, nor solicited the avowal of.

92.

If a book is well written, I always find it too short.

93.

Silly things do cease to be silly if they are done by sensible people in an impudent way.

94.

I must learn to be content with being happier than I deserve.

95.

If things are going untowardly one month, they are sure to mend the next.

96.

Better be without sense than misapply it as you do.

97.

Nobody can tell what I suffer! But it is always so. Those who do not complain are never pitied.

98.

But to appear happy when I am so miserable Oh! who can require it?

99.

Time will generally lessen the interest of every attachment not within the daily circle.

100.

You have qualities which I had not before supposed to exist in such a degree in any human creature. You have some touches of the angel in you.

Made in United States
North Haven, CT
21 November 2021